LOOK UP

Cescyia Stevenson

Look Up

Look Up
Cescyia Stevenson
ISBN: 9781736745533
Copyright ©2021 by Cescyia Stevenson
All rights reserved. No part of this book may be reproduced in any form whatsoever, including information storage and retrieval systems, without permission in writing from the author—exceptions by reviewers, who may quote brief passages in a book review.

Edited by Shawn Jackson
Cover by Design Place LLC
Published by One2Mpower Publishing LLC

Cescyia Stevenson

Acknowledgements

God, thank you for giving me the gift of writing. You could have given anyone the gifts you gave to me, but I am thankful you entrusted me to carry out every kingdom assignment you gave me. To my family, friends, church family, and healthcare professionals, thank you so much for all the extended love, support, and wisdom God spoke through you that helped me overcome many obstacles. I cannot repay you, but I love you all!

A special thank you to Sandra Daniel, Clara M. Sowers, Allison, Katasha Acosta, Letha Denise, Coretta D., Evonne J., Landy Patterson, Malissa C., Von Gretchen, and Kamal M. Thank you for being the balance I needed during this process.

Look Up

To my grandmother, Essie Stevenson, thank you for pouring so much into me as God allowed you to do. Your courage helped me understand God's true love towards His children. I am thankful God allowed me to walk with you through your journey until the day you gained your heavenly wings. Your love for me will never be forgotten.

Cescyia Stevenson

Preface

As I started this book, I wanted to tell my story from the perspective of Naomi and Ruth from the Bible. I looked at the fact that Ruth was a caregiver just like me, and she had little just like me. Ruth had a heart to not only help Naomi, but she wanted to learn more about the God whom Naomi trusted in. I believe Ruth got weary sometimes and was not sure how things would turn out. The book of 1 Timothy 5:3-5 challenges believers to look after their family members who are widows and take care of them. For many years, I had exercised this scripture by helping many elderly people in my neighborhood. I recall a family member trying to downplay the fact that I was helping the elderly because I was young, and there were other things I could do with my time. As I look back, I noticed that God was training me for this season, and he was giving me the heart to be able to do it with ease.

When God brought me back home to Florida, I thought it would be short-lived. But little did I know, He was answering my prayers. So often, we pray and even plead with God, and then he not only shows up with an answer, but it is the appointed time to walk out God's plan. I asked God to help me to be in a position where I could continue to work and help my grandmother. I had prayed this prayer because my grandmother was having some health issues, and I thought I needed to be with her to help her through the process. This book shares my experience as my grandmother's caregiver. I truly pray you, as the reader, can get something out of my experience.

Look Up

Cescyia Stevenson

CHAPTER 1

Writing a story about something that is close to your heart can be challenging, especially when you have an opportunity to be transparent. I thought about everything I had gone through personally as my grandmother's caregiver. My emotions were all over the place at times, and when things would get "hot in the kitchen," I had to learn to look up. It was so easy for people to say trust in God and believe that everything was taken care of. I knew all of this because, in a season in my life, I lived those words out. This was a different season, and I was in a different mental space. I would be faking if I told you it was glory hallelujah all the time. There were times when I felt alone, and often, I would shed tears because I felt like I should have been doing more. I needed to embrace God's love that would allow me to hold my head up and know He was truly with me.

Sometimes, what you see in front of you can change the way you respond to certain situations down the road.

In May 2011, God answered my prayer of going to graduate school to further my education. The company I worked for at the time had several opportunities to travel overseas, but I was not able to travel because one person was out on leave, and of course, I had my graduate classes. After I successfully completed my Master's in Business Management (Executive Leadership) in 2012, my director at the time gave me the green light that I could start traveling. I went on my first trip in the fall of 2012. I was extremely nervous about flying overseas because I was more concerned about flying over a large body of water, but I got over my fear once I landed in Dubai. In early 2013, I went back on a long-term assignment that lasted until the start of summer.

After I returned to the states, I noticed there were some significant organizational changes. The vice president of my group left the organization, and then new senior-level executives started to come in. When my projects started being reassigned to other colleagues, I knew at that time my days were numbered. As I looked at the organizational chart that would be effective January 1, 2014, I saw my position was eliminated, and my temporary position supporting the senior-level executives was coming to an end. God prepared me with the strategy I needed to survive from January to June 2014. When I was released from my job, I was not hurt about losing my position, but I did not like being called out of my character.

Look Up

As the vice president of human resources sat in front of me with a smirk on her face, I knew what God had shown me all along, "A person without a vision will always mismanage valuable resources because he or she is unable to look beyond the deficiencies to get to the hidden gems." I knew that day when I left her days were numbered. When I was informed three months after my release, she had been released from the company; I was not surprised at all. I saw the warning signs she ignored. I worked for another organization for about a month, and God closed the doors where I was, and I headed back home.

God will always provide a strategy to help you get through challenging times.

My prayer of taking care of my grandmother came to fruition in August 2014. I landed a couple of contract assignments, and after the second one, God truly cleared the way so I could focus on my new assignment. There were many challenges I faced early on in caring for my grandmother. In those challenging times, I had to learn to look up. God placed me in the position of ministering to a person who needed a reminder of who He was.

As I entered this season of caregiving, I thought I knew what I was getting into. As a matter of fact, I thought I was doing the same thing I had done before. To my surprise, I entered a season of breaking, reshaping, and molding. When one starts a new journey, he or she assumes everything presented should be easy, but one should count the cost. Luke 14:28 (KJV) states, "For which of you, intending to build a tower, sitteth not down first, and counteth the cost, whether he have sufficient to finish it?" Many people will jump feet first into the pool before considering how deep the water is. I recall, as a child, I would not go into the deep end of the pool because my feet did not touch the bottom of the pool. Touching the bottom of the pool gave me confidence and security I would not drown. Often God wants us to launch into the deep just so we will know how strong He is in us (2 Corinthians 12:9).

Point #1 Your Prayers Matter to God!

James 5:16 (KJV) reminds us as believers the effectual, fervent prayers of a righteous man availeth much.

When we consistently pray and seek God, the end results remind us of God's faithfulness towards us. Go back in time and think about the petitions you made to God and what was the outcome. If you are in tune with God, you will see how everything works together for your good (Romans 8:28). My grandmother understood the power of prayer, and she never stopped using this tool. For three nights straight at the same time during her final transition, she would say the Lord's prayer, and she would make emphasis on, "forgive our debts, as we forgive our debtors" (Matthew 6:12, KJV). It was at this point I knew she was reconciling with God. She wanted to be sure she would be able to lay at the feet of Jesus.

Look Up

CHAPTER 2

During 2015 the breaking started to happen. I watched as my grandmother started spitting up the insides of her stomach (bile), and she stopped eating and drinking. The hospice nurse tried to help me to understand what was going on, but it was a lot to take in. As her friends were dying, and she was calling out their names it seemed like she desired to be with them. An old wife's tale said, if your loved one starts to call out family members or friends who have died, that is a sign they may be dying. Yes, it became scary for me, but I had to learn how to pray a little harder.

It was a challenge for me to wrap my mind around the unknown. I reached out to several friends who encouraged me to really trust God. Seeing my grandmother spit up a

Look Up

yellow fluid her doctor referred to as bile, and then hearing the doctor saying my grandmother was at the end of her life did not sit well with me. Although death visited her, it was not time for her to go. I cried out to God, and He heard me and answered (Psalm 120:1). Thinking about planning a funeral for your loved one is hard, especially when you are close to them. The hospice nurses were incredibly supportive and explained things to my uncle and me. BUT ONE DAY, around three in the afternoon, my grandmother woke up. She started talking to God and repenting, forgiving people for the things she had done to others. I recall her telling God she was sorry for not being faithful to Him and she would do better. The next thing I knew, she was praising God, and I felt a shift in the atmosphere. In Ezekiel chapter 37, the story of the dry bones began to unfold in my grandmother's life as God breathed on her again, and she went from almost dying to be fully refreshed.

After my younger brother died in February 2016, I returned to graduate school online to pursue a master's in business administration (MBA) with a focus in leadership. I continued to care for my grandmother, and in December, she celebrated her ninetieth birthday. Although I was supposed to complete my degree in December, I had to take an additional term to complete one class. I was not happy about that. One of my friends encouraged me during this time and told me, "Enjoy the process. You're almost there." Those words helped me to get through eight weeks' worth of assignments. In March 2017, I received my degree, and things would begin to shift in my grandmother's life. As Thanksgiving approached, my grandmother started down the road she was on in 2015. She started like she

Look Up

was drifting away. The thought of losing her did not feel well at all.

I began to cry out to God, and He heard me. God reminded me of Hezekiah in 2 Kings 2:1-6. Hezekiah was told by the prophet he was going to die. Hezekiah turned his face to the wall and prayed, and God answered and extended his life fifteen years. Those were words of encouragement I needed. As I began to talk to my grandmother about how scared I was of her leaving, she started setting me straight. When I told her how I looked up all her symptoms online, and everything pointed towards death because of the information that was provided by hospice, she told me, "I told you about being on that Internet all the time. I am not dying anytime soon because I still have work to do. When it is my time to go, it will just be my time." Then she asked me to sit on the side of her bed. She looked me directly in my eyes and told me, "Trust God." Yes, I knew to trust God, but in a short moment, my humanly emotions had taken over. It happens to the best of us, but that was a moment when God reminded me of Isaiah 53:1, "Whose report will you believe." That was a moment I needed to understand I had to live what I was reading and speaking. My grandmother's life was extended an additional nine months.

Something to consider...

We are our environment. We must be careful of the things we entertain or allow to come into the environment our loved one lives in. Words are powerful and can change the atmosphere. The information the nurses were providing me during my grandmother's last nine months was helpful. There were times when they would say she was starting to transition. Transition simply means someone is at the end of their life, and they are not expected to live. It was easy to reject what the nurses were saying because it came off as being negative to me. However, I had to learn I was in the learning process, and the hospice nurses had more knowledge in this area. My primary goal was to make sure my grandmother's environment was filled with God's love, peace, and words of life were always spoken.

Point #2 Trust God

Psalm 56:3 (NKJV) Whenever I am afraid, I will trust in You.

My grandmother's trust in God came from years of dealing with people who would take from her and even take advantage of her. Some of the people would even brag about how much they loved her, but their actions towards her did not show God's love. As my grandmother would share stories of the things people would do and how she responded, I saw God's true love lived on the inside of her. She never wanted me to get to the point that I depended on her or others to the point that I forgot about God. That was one lesson I learned quickly and hid in my heart.

CHAPTER 3

As my grandmother celebrated her last birthday on earth, she enjoyed a cake my sister designed and close family around her. In March of 2018, pneumonia surfaced again, and she conquered it. God began to pour into her more, and she would closely follow the instructions He would give to her. Many people were blessed because of her obedience. While all of this was happening, the cancerous tumor was pushing out and draining. There was a time during this journey that my grandmother would say, "I am healed. No more cancer." But there was a day when my grandmother told me the cancer was back. This tumor started out like a golf ball in 2009, and it shrunk while she was taking a hormone pill. It was a small knot until the end of 2017, and that is when it started to grow. God had been faithful to her.

During my grandmother's ups and downs, she would say different things. One of the things she said was, "I am getting a new roof on my house." I smiled and said, "Okay," thinking to myself, God is speaking through her. Days before her body started transitioning, she received that new roof. On August 21, I had no idea what I was about to face. This day would change my life forever.

My grandmother and I had a routine every day. I would clean her up and then read the Bible and pray with her. Sometimes, I would sing a few songs because it would lift her spirit. Just like we feed our natural bodies, our loved ones need spiritual nourishment to survive. Your loved one needs to hear the word of God every day, just like you do! Reading Bible stories and praying with your loved ones will go a long

Look Up

way. My grandmother complained about her stomach feeling bad, so I gave her some medicine to help her with it. We had gone on an "as needed" basis with her medication because some of the medicine would cause different effects. For example, one medication caused her heart rate to go up in a matter of minutes. Another medicine would cause her to sleep for hours. The medicine I gave her for her stomach caused what appeared to be a sleeping reaction. God led me to read Deuteronomy 15:1-6, a passage that talked about the year of the Lord's release. Her spirit was in communication with God, and as I began to explain to her that she was debt-free, I noticed a change. When her personal care assistant came to see her, that is when her body started shutting down. My grandmother's body turned cold as ice. Her nurse had to be called, and oxygen had to be ordered. Normally, my grandmother would not agree about being hooked up to an oxygen machine, but this time was different. I thought pneumonia had shown back up according to the symptoms she stated to display, but death had arrived at her door.

Point #3 Faith Walk

2 Corinthians 5:7(KJV) For we walk by faith and not by sight.

When my grandmother started an all-girls softball team for our neighborhood, it was a faith walk. She was able to obtain a vacant field in the neighborhood and sponsorships to help support the needs of the team. The people in my community were proud of the girl's team, and it even inspired another person in the community to petition for a pavilion to be added right next to the field. The Pierce Bombers and Agrico Aggies became one of the best accomplishments of her life.

When the end of my grandmother's life approached, I realized that I needed God like never before. I had to truly walk by faith in what would be her final days. When my grandmother fell in 2013 and had to have surgery for a pinched nerve, she told me she had a talked with the Master, and he told her, if she had the surgery, she would live. In hindsight, when she experienced end of life moments like this, those experiences were merely practice rounds for me.

On August 23, my grandmother told me she was almost at the river to cross, and she was extremely excited about it. The term "river to cross" means that a person who is going through his or her final life transition is near death, and it is only a matter of time before he or she dies. I took time to allow God to speak through me. I told my grandmother a story about a runner in a race. I told her not to be in a rush to finish the race but rather pace herself all the way until the end. I told her not everyone runs at the same speed, and it may seem that some people may finish before you, but do not get discouraged; stay in the race. Then my grandmother had her moment and told me, "Never give up." For the next few days, she would struggle with death. She even asked me to help her to live. I asked her some important questions, "Do you feel God needs you to do something else? Are you worried about…? and I named several people." When I got to my name, that is when she told me how concerned she was about my future. This was a serious moment in the conversation that I could not be selfish but rather remind her of how God took care of her and assure her He would do the same for me. I knew like before, God could give me the strategy, but I asked her did she ask God about her desire to live. Her facial expression was priceless because her answer was no.

As I called everyone to tell them the news, she got anxious to leave. I recall her telling one of her sons, "Bubba, I am leaving and

Look Up

not coming back," with a big smile on her face. Being able to see some of her family members that she had not seen in a long time gave her the peace she needed. I could tell on that Friday she was mad with God because she was still alive, and she wanted to be gone. I had to have that mother-to-child conversation with her because she needed to understand God was going to honor her heart's desire. When she finally got to see her sister after many years, she was so excited that she used up a lot of strength to tell her she loved her. It was hard to explain to my aunt that my grandmother was passing, but I believe she got it. She said her last goodbye to her daughter, and her organs began to shut down further. On that Sunday, everything that was in her digestive system started to come out. I said out loud, "Who gave you a laxative in your oxygen tank!"

Around one fifty a.m. on Tuesday, August 28, I checked on her for the last time before I went to bed. Hours later, when my uncle, her son, went to check on her, he said, "You need to call the people (hospice)," because she is gone. It was ten minutes to seven a.m., and my big baby was gone. It had been a week since she started the transition, and I had already asked God to give me the peace I needed to get through handling everything.

Thank God my grandmother had already planned everything. I mean, she would not stop getting on me about getting her grave spot and talking to the funeral home. Even though I felt scared doing all of this, God brought me to a place of peace with her final preparation. As my family began to prepare for her funeral, I became more appreciative that everything was done, except for a few things. She picked out her suit, and one of her daughters provided a hat. My big baby was dressed like a missionary, ready for her next mission.

The beauty we have in life is the ability to prepare for the unknown while continuing to live a life filled with God's love, peace, and hope. Hebrews 11:1 reminds us that "faith is the substance of things hoped for and the evidence of things not seen." People can hope for great things to come out of the life they lived here on earth, but it is not until after a person dies that you see their true legacy. We should live a life that is pleasing unto God so that the life we lived here on earth will reflect the true reward we expect in the end.

Cescyia Stevenson

CHAPTER 4

I referred to the story of Ruth and Naomi so many times during the latter part of my assignment because I could identify with what was going through Naomi and Ruth's mind. It was hard for Naomi to accept the fact that God was allowing Ruth to help her because she felt Ruth could marry again and have a brand-new life. My grandmother was no different than Naomi. She felt I should have been enjoying life without having to change the diaper of an elderly person. What my grandmother did not realize was my heart and mind were fixed on doing what God asked of me to do. I was not interested in doing anything else.

The question you may ask yourself is, "How does a person get to the point that he or she has the mindset of Ruth?" When an individual decides to deeply commit all their ways unto God (Psalm 37:5), then and only then will the person fully be able to have the mindset Ruth had. Many people only commit to God's plan only when it seems like they will benefit from it. I had nothing to lose from taking care of my grandmother.

Naomi had to also commit to God's plan and recognize the assignment that was before her. God used my grandmother to help me to overcome disappointments and to truly recognize how people really felt about me. There were things I saw while living far away, and now that I was up close and personal with those things, I began to understand why there were so many emotional roller coasters in my life. It was time to let some people go and move forward with my life. This process resembles Orpah going back home while Ruth moved forward with Naomi.

Look Up

People have a time and season in your life, and sometimes we allow people to stay longer than God intended. My grandmother had to learn certain people were not able to walk with her during certain phases of her life because they were not equipped to help her in the long run. There were also other people God allowed to do different things for my grandmother, but even those doors began to close. Getting close to God requires all distractions to be moved out of the way, so we can focus on what he needs from us.

So often, we hold our heads down because we are ashamed of the decisions we made. We even hold our heads down because we do not feel worthy of receiving something, we felt we did not deserve. Psalm 121:1-2 tells us to look to the hills from whence cometh our help, our help cometh from the Lord. When God helps us, He expects nothing back. My grandmother could not understand why I was sticking with her throughout her process. God would always speak through me to remind her he had not forgotten all the times she took care of others. Our loved ones need to be reminded how important they are to God. Naomi wanted to change her name to Marah, meaning bitter because of the things that happened to her. My grandmother needed to hear that God hadn't forgotten how much she labored with her loved ones during their time of need.

The unconditional love my grandmother gave out to others, God poured back into her. As a caregiver it was tough at times trying to explain why family and close friends weren't calling or visiting. Sometimes it would be uncomfortable, but God helped me through it. Many people wondered how I survived four years of taking care of my grandmother with a limited social life. It was God. I had to learn to look up to Him in every area of my life. God pulled out of me everything He poured into me over the years. It was not a coincidence God had me living with my grandmother from a baby and then off and on until my teenage years, in which He allowed me to stay with her full time.

God's purpose of me taking care of her in my younger days came full circle in her time of need. It may seem like I am repeating myself with a few things, but just know that God takes the foolish things and confound the wise (1 Corinthians 1:27). What does it mean to look up? Looking up simply means an individual is not allowing a situation or circumstance to control their emotions to the point that he or she becomes depressed. Depression and oppression are real! As a caregiver, one can either have one of those emotions or even both. As Bible-based believers, we are challenged in our everyday walk to live out the word of God we say we believe in.

Cescyia Stevenson

Even now, post my grandmother's death, I am still challenged by some of the things I faced before. People asking what is next and how are you going to survive. A friend encouraged me with this, "Stay strong, cleave to God." I have had to hold close to this. I know Ruth's family probably had multiple options for her, but she chose to follow her heart. It has been hard following my heart, but every time God has brought all the details together. I have learned to keep my mouth shut and not give out too many details because not everyone has your best interest. Through my experience as a caregiver, I had to learn not to be naïve about the things God was showing me about people. As Jesus interacted with different people, he knew who was for him and who was against him. Sometimes we can discern who is really for us, and other times, our emotions lead us wrong.

Look Up

CHAPTER 5

Something to remember—many elderly people began to see their family members at face value when they lose their independence. Of course, many of them noticed their family members' character based upon their interactions over the years, and they hope that the person would possibly change. Our loved ones are looking for a person or people who will be supportive when he or she loses his or her independence. There were certain things God showed me during my caregiving time. When our independence is taken away, then our attitude changes.

When Naomi accepted Ruth coming back to her homeland with her, she accepted the fact God was allowing Ruth to return to help her. My grandmother loved the short-term help she was receiving from myself and other family

Look Up

members. But after a while, it became old, and she started getting agitated because what she would normally do on her own a certain way was no longer happening. It got to the point that each person specialized in doing certain things for her. Most elderly people try to maintain their independence because they do not want to bother their family members. Sometimes elderly people suffer from silent depression, and they will find things to keep busy to overshadow the fact that they miss interacting with their family. Interaction with family members, telling old stories, and sharing old family recipes helps the elderly cope with the fact that things in their world have significantly changed. God has given me the heart for the elderly. I can be in the store, and I will help as many elderly people as possible that God will allow me to help. It brings joy, peace, and comfort in knowing someone who may be overlooked is receiving the help he or she needs.

Naomi's had an attitude change about life. After losing her husband and her sons wasting their inheritance in Moab, Naomi had nothing, and she had to wrap her mind around what was next for her. You may personally face a time in your life where it seems like you have lost everything and there is nothing to hope for, just know there is hope. My grandmother went through urinary tract infections (UTIs), dementia, arthritis, and other symptoms from breast cancer. The changes my grandmother went through caused me to be challenged mentally and spiritually. There were times when I became exhausted, and God was the only one who could replenish what I poured out. At one point, I had a life coach who helped remind me about my goals in life. It was easy to become comfortable in a temporary situation, especially when you do not plan. My life coach helped me

Look Up

to move forward after losing a job and even almost losing my grandmother early on.

The demand from taking care of your loved one can go from being minor to major within a set time. Instead of doing things in a routine way all the time, open yourself up to being asked like a kid to do something right then and there. You will find out your loved one wants things done now and not a minute later. If you are not used to being demanded to do something, then you will need to prep yourself for that day. You will get agitated when your loved one demands you give them all your attention, especially when you are looking to do something for yourself. Just like a child who has something to say when his or her mother gets on the phone, your loved one will have the same behavior.

Checking your attitude and how you deal with your loved one should be something you do very often. The more you recognize their condition is driving their behavior, the better off you will be. I had to ask God many times to help me adjust my attitude to be the best servant I could be. I will say there are some people who are just mean because they hoard unforgiveness and pride in their hearts. The bitterness that is deep within their hearts causes them to live a life of silent shame and guilt. God does not want his children to live life like this.

Look Up

CHAPTER 6

I want to close by saying my journey was not easy. I had to live 1 Corinthians 13:4 (ERV), "Love suffereth long, and is kind..." The rejection as a baby, child, and even parts of my adult life showed me how self-centered people could be. Being around my grandmother during the last four years of her life allowed me to deal with rejection head-on. When my grandmother and I would talk about things that happened in her life, I could see she too dealt with rejection. It hurt her, but she made moving forward look so easy.

I wondered how a woman who went through a couple of failed marriages and abuse could encourage me not to look at the infraction but love unconditionally. It started to be clear—I needed to look up! My

Look Up

grandmother's dependence on God helped her to help those who did her wrong with a loving heart. That set her apart from so many people I had encountered before. I can honestly say I have lived the same lifestyle of treating others with love and kindness and not anger and strife. My trust and faith in God became a lot stronger when I started letting go of the hurt, shame, and pain. I am still a work in progress, but I am not where I used to be.

If you do not get anything out of this book, I want you to be encouraged that your life story has a purpose. The things you have experienced over the years will come in full circle. The people in your life will change but embrace those whom God sends to help you. I prayed for many things over the years, and even in this assignment as a caregiver, my prayer was answered. You see I have prayed for things to happen a certain way, and life has taken me on a detour. God wants you to know you need to rest in him. Matthew 11:28-30, "Come to me, all you who are weary and burdened, and I will give you rest. Take my yoke upon you and learn from me, for I am gentle and humble in heart, and you will find rest for your souls. For my yoke is easy and my burden is light." When we allow God to take care of everything, we are not in a position of worry.

Isaiah 61:3 (NKJV) also reminds us, "To put on the garment of praise for the spirit of heaviness." Heaviness can stem from having a hard time believing God specializes in the impossible. Seeing other people's failures often deters us from wanting more in life. For many years, I fought mentally, back and forth, whether I wanted certain things in life. Until one day, I had to ask myself whether I was going to continue to live a doubleminded life or not. I asked God to help take what I saw as normal and destroy those thoughts and replace them with his truth. God wants to direct our

Look Up

paths (Proverbs 3:6), so we can get the best out of life. I cannot get my grandmother back, but I can use the wisdom she imparted in me to move forward in life.

Cescyia Stevenson

About the Author

Cescyia Stevenson is a licensed evangelist who has traveled to several countries while working in the government sector. Throughout her life, she has made it her mission to be a light in a dark place. Cescyia earned her undergraduate degree from the University of Florida in Television and Film Production and two master's degrees: Business Executive Leadership and MBA from Liberty University. After working in the government sector for seven years, Cescyia started caring for her grandmother full-time in 2014 until she passed in 2018. After her grandmother's passing, Cescyia returned to the educational field and has been using her life experiences to help troubled youth to get back on track. It is Cescyia's mission to share the Gospel of Jesus Christ to as many people as she can through her writing and productions.

www.ingramcontent.com/pod-product-compliance
Lightning Source LLC
Chambersburg PA
CBHW021001090426
42736CB00010B/1408